Brian has been one of my pivotal influences in critical thinking about life goals, and how to get from point A to point B, while maintaining health, sanity and thriving relationships with those close to me. With so little time, and so many factors in life that we don't control, it's important to know how to use the tools and time we have both efficiently and effectively to make the life we live matter - to us and to others, Brian has helped me do that. As a songwriter/producer, I have made crucial changes to the way I work that lead to days I enjoy and accomplishments I can be proud of. There's a long haul ahead of me, but taking advice from Brian Stegner shifts perspective from the journey being daunting to it being exciting!

JOEY LANGLOIS

Songwriter, Producer; WhatIfElephants.com

In America, there's a widespread sickness - workaholism - that's glorified as the ultimate professional milestone. It took productivity gurus like Brian Stegner to help me embrace a more productive, more minimalistic lifestyle. Brian has an à la Tim Ferris work methodology that I've put into practice in most of my recent endeavours, whether in my business coaching or personal investments. Why work 80 hours when you can slash that by 3, all the while living a fuller life focused on the essentials? Brian has helped me rethink business, and I now help companies around the world doing just that with Espresso Coaching. You don't necessarily need more resources, you need a shot of Espresso: less is more!

SEBASTIEN LEDUC

Managing Partner, EspressoCoaching.com

If I think about it...I realize that most of the productivity skills I have developed over the last seven years have come as a result of Brian Stegner's work. He is a practitioner as well as a teacher. You would do well to devour this book and implement these principles into your life as fast as you can - because Stegner will keep cranking out better ways to do things!

DWIGHT BERNIER

Director for Acts 29 Canada;

Author of ONE: A Gospel Guide to Pre-Marriage Counseling

When it comes to putting ideas to work, efficiently, the first person I'd turn to is Brian Stegner. If you want to do something well and you want to do it quickly, see how Brian Stegner is doing it. For years I have watched Brian Stegner do significantly more than most people with seemingly less effort. He knows how to do many things well, to do them quickly, and somehow he continues to increase his efficiency. Brian is someone I'd turn to for help in a range of subjects, but efficiency in execution of tasks more than any other.

MIKE GOCKLEY

Director of Leadership Development, Church 21

Brian is one of those guys that, when you start to realize how many plates he actually has spinning, you simply go 'Wow!' The old adage about if you want something done, ask a busy person certainly applies here. Brian has never, in my experience with him, failed to deliver exactly what was asked on-time and almost always much better than I asked. When you ask him how he does it, he simply smiles his bearded all-knowing smile. Here are some of his ninja secrets of executing quickly and efficiently. Prepare to take the red pill and hang on... it's going to be an amazing ride.

DAVID LONG

Continuous Improvement Manager
in a Forbes Global 2000 Company

Brian's easily the most efficient person I've ever met. Working alongside him for the past six years, I've seen him solve problems with quick, creative solutions nearly as many times as I've seen him meditate on something for a couple of days and come back with a brilliant plan to optimize workflow. If anybody knows how to hack life and make it run smoother, it's Brian Stegner. I wouldn't be where I am today if I hadn't spent this much time being inspired to work even half as hard as he does.

TOM ZALATNAI

Executive Producer, UpfordNetwork.com

One of the best experiences I had while living in Montreal was meeting Brian. His friendship, wisdom, and observing firsthand the sheer volume of creative work he accomplishes on a daily basis left an indelible impression in my life. Over the past 10 years working as a Program Manager in the aerospace and manufacturing industries, I have learned productivity is an indispensable skill-set intrinsic to the discipline of Program and Project Management in order to execute successfully. The approach and concepts Brian has shared with me over the years have been invaluable to my profession as a Program Manager as well as my personal life. I am excited he has decided to put his ideas succinctly in a book and hope his words will help engender confidence in bringing order from chaos in people's everyday lives.

EMILIO RIVERA

Program Manager in the Aerospace & Manufacturing Industries

If you're looking to move your business, non-profit, or life goals into warp-speed without burning out look no further! Brian has mastered the art of a productive life without the nasty side-effects. I have benefited from his life hacks for years and now, in his newest book, so can you.

ANDY STEIGER

Founder & Director of Apologetics Canada;
Author of Thinking?: Answering Life's Five Biggest Questions

SCARY FAST

7 Advanced Hacks to Boost Your Productivity 1,000x

BRIAN MICHAEL STEGNER

Published by Thunderbox Digital
CP80030 Principale
Chateauguay, QC J6J 5X2
Canada

Second Print Edition - 2022 v2.0

© 2022 Brian Michael Stegner. All rights reserved. No portion of this book may be reproduced in any form without permission from the publisher, except as permitted by U.S. copyright law. For permissions contact:

permissions@thunderboxdigitial.com

ISBN: 9781980569589

Visit the author's website at BrianMichaelStegner.com

I am deeply grateful for all of the people I have had a chance to work with over the last few years, many of whom so kindly provided me with the commendations that are printed at the start of this book. I have learned a great deal from each of you and you deserve your own share of the credit for what's in these pages.

I would also like to thank my wife who, on some level, probably wishes that she hadn't married someone with a rocket on their back, and yet who has been a tireless encouragement to me in all of my many ventures.

Soli Deo gloria

Contents

Warning	XIII
Required Prerequisites	XV
Introduction	3
Basic Skills Review	11
Hack #1	25
Hack #2	35
Hack #3	47
Hack #4	57
Hack #5	69
Hack #6	83
Hack #7	95
Epilogue	109

Warning

THIS IS NOT YOUR USUAL PRODUCTIVITY BOOK

Most productivity books available today focus on helping you learn how to accomplish things by overcoming your mental blocks, fears, and in some cases, simple laziness. You can think of these as being like Productivity 101 classes. They're important, and if you haven't read any of them you probably should. They'll help you learn how to DO things and how to do MORE things, both important skills.

But this book isn't about that stuff.

Instead, this book is about doing things *faster*. And not faster as in,

"Wow, I'm getting so much done today!"

Or even,

"Yikes, what do I do now that I've finished everything I can think of..."

But like,

OPERATOR: "911, what's your emergency?"

YOU: "...CAN'T....STOP....ACCOMPLSHING!"

You get the idea: It isn't about being Fast, being Very Fast, or even being Stupid Fast.

It's about being SCARY Fast.

You might *die* fast.

So, fair warning:

Read at your own risk.

Required Prerequisites

IF OTHER PRODUCTIVITY BOOKS are "101", *Scary Fast* is designed to be like "201, 301, 401, and 501" level courses in Productivity, e.g., the *Advanced* Courses. And like in all advanced courses, there are mandatory prerequisites. In order to benefit from *Scary Fast*, it is assumed that you already have a basic understanding of:

1. How to get things done.

2. Organizational skills.

If you don't have those basic skills down, well...this probably isn't the book for you.

Would you enter a powerlifting contest without first spending at least a few months in the gym training with a knowledgeable coach? Of course not.

You'd blow out your spine in a blaze of glory.

In the same way, these hacks can mess up your life if you're not already fairly organized and able to deal with basic task accomplishment. Find someone who knows you and loves you and ask them to be brutally honest about your productivity and organizational skills. Heed their advice, and if you're not ready, come back when you are.

Go ahead, I'll wait...

Still reading? You realize that this section is basically a thinly veiled *warning #2* to "not read this unless you're ready"?...

No one seems to take these warnings seriously.

(Sigh)

I guess it's safe for you to at least read the introduction...

You don't have to do anything you don't want to do.

- David Harold Fink

Introduction

It's 1998 and I'm sitting in a college classroom in Chicago, taking some kind of personality test. There are maybe thirty people in the room, and we're all scribbling away furiously at our questionnaires. Eventually the professor stops us and instructs us to plot our answers on an X and Y kind of thing, all drawn out in a square grid. I end up having to add two more squares by hand to the lower left quadrant so I can plot where I landed. Frowning at my hand-drawn modification of their obviously insufficient scoring tool, I vaguely hear the professor ask us, "Now move to the desk in the classroom relative to where you are positioned on the scoring chart."

We all stand and shuffle to our new seats, dictated by our neurological makeup.

As I migrate to the metal desk / chair combo at the back left of the classroom (about opposite of where the door to the hall is), I look at my chart for reference and realize I'm going to have to move the desk. I begin scraping the WWII era, all-metal assembly across the hardwood floors towards the classroom window.

Unable to actually get to where I am "supposed to be" according to the chart I had plotted, I accept a position next to the window, hugging the wall, and take my seat. It is at this moment that I choose to look up and as I do so, I see the rest of the classroom, including the professor, staring at me.

In my single-minded focus upon accomplishing the task at hand, I had failed to notice that I was the *only person* that had moved to the back left quadrant of the classroom *at all*. That I had just isolated myself from the group, and *then* effectively spent the next thirty seconds noisily moving myself even further away, as far away as I could possibly get from the other humans in the room.

Unsure of myself in social situations at that point in my life, I didn't automatically generate some kind of witty quip designed to make me look cool and assuage the masses. Instead I kept silent and looked at the authority figure to break the tension. He asked me, "Are you where you're supposed to be seated according to your results?"

I looked at the chart on my desk, and then out the window.

"I'm actually supposed to be a few more feet out this way, but...the wall..." I mumble.

The classroom was very quiet. My answer was not reassuring. They all now looked at the professor, waiting for him to send me out of the room for being different, or perhaps whip a tranquilizer dart out of his jacket pocket and put me down before I could metamorphosize into my true form and fly out the window in a explosion of glass fragments and twisted metal window frames.

Nothing like this happened though. Instead he turned to address the rest of the class and said that it was "normal" that in a group of about this size, there would usually be one of "these" (referring to me). And then he went around the classroom in a clockwise motion, pointing at each group in turn:

"These people come up with ideas." (Smiles from that section.)

"This group figures out how to do them." (Serious nods from the "STEM" students.)

"These people back here just like to have fun." (Cheers from the party-people.)

"And then this guy..." (turning to point at me) "...90% of what gets done in the world is done by people like him."

(No response on my part, other than to avoid the eye contact of everyone else.)

I have forgotten most of the rest of what happened that day...it was probably occluded by the brilliant light of the personal revelation experience I had when the professor named me for what I secretly was: a doer.

Fast-forward to today, I now know that I'm something called an INTJ, and an off-the-charts one at that (literally so in case of the test I took back in that classroom). If you're versed in the parlance of the Myers-Briggs personality typing system, you're already picking out that I'm Introverted (the "I" in INTJ) which means that I draw my energy from task-accomplishment and information gathering (versus people-time like an Extrovert would). As a result my natural state is to be at-work, and it's difficult for me to be at-rest.

Therein is part of the reason that INTJ's get so much done, just being Introverted stacks the deck in your favor. You kind of can't help but get a lot done because it feels good / replenishes energies spent in being with other people.

But there is so much more to it than that for my type; those other three letters (NTJ) end up taking my tasking to a whole new level. More than just being Introverted, INTJ's have a *unique way* that our brains interact with tasks, a basket of stuff like prioritizing, maximizing, batching, overlapping, cross-training, synergizing, all of which come naturally, without being intentional or even really conscious of it.

It wasn't until later, when I discovered and read the "4 Hour Work Week" by Tim Ferriss, and learned about things like the 80 / 20 Principle and Parkinson's Law (both of which I'll define in the next few chapters) that I realized there were *names* for some of the ways that I worked.

It also allowed me to review how I use these principles in a more objective manner and maximize my utilization of them.*

*Picture gas being poured on a fire and you get some idea of the impact of that book on my life.

My brain quickly took those principles way beyond their average utilization and made up NEW principles that were even more productive, and dangerously so. My productivity hockey-sticked from already being wildly above average to life-threatening. It was probably like the feeling that guy had who had strapped those solid-state fuel rockets to the top of his car. Amazing for about five seconds, white-knuckled terror for the remainder of the trip.

(Spoiler - He died.)

I didn't die (thankfully) though it was some time before I got things back under control. It's not like I could UNLEARN or UN-FIGURE-OUT those things that my brain had started to do. This information was dangerous for me. I started getting things done WAY TOO FAST, and as a result doing WAY TOO MUCH. Balance was lost.

It was about that time that the panic attacks started. The sheer mass of what I had set in motion all at the same time was terrifying to contemplate.

After several months of aggressive deceleration, I managed to get my life back.

Wiser, I learned that there is such a thing as being TOO productive, and I began looking for means of putting these new principles into practice in ways that allowed my life more freedom, not less.

The end result is that I now have a set of skills that allow me to hit a Big Red Button and get things done at an unprecedented rate, but also the self-discipline to only push the button when I'm ready and able to accept the consequences, and have the controls in place to survive.

This book will help you to build that Big Red Button in your own mind. And as with all red buttons, once it's there, you can't take it away. (Thinly veiled *warning #3*.) It'll be up to you to live with that red button and NOT push it unless you really need to. You will have to exercise a measure of self-control. I take no responsibility for what may happen if you decide to read what comes next.

Some of us are like wheelbarrows, only useful when pushed and easily upset.

- Jack Herbert

Basic Skills Review

IT'S 1999 AND I'M returning a stack of Science Fiction novels to the college library, and checking out a new stack of equal weight. The librarian looks over her glasses at the two piles and then at my face.

"Are you actually *reading* these?..."

I think she suspected I was just using them to build forts in my dorm room or to plan a bank heist. In her defense, I had been checking out a pile of books like this on a weekly basis for a month now.

It was unnatural.

"I've finished all my assignments," I mumble.

With only this wildly unbelievable explanation to work with, the librarian reluctantly allowed me to leave with a new armload of books.

But I was telling the truth. I had arrived a week early to my second year because my girlfriend at the time was a first-year and needed to be there for orientation week. In retrospect, I realized I should have gone to orientation also. I was a transfer student (from that school in Chicago I previously mentioned) and I ended up not knowing where anything was or how anything worked. But instead of sitting through all of that boring stuff I went around and got all of my syllabuses from my professors (who were also skipping orientation and had nothing to do during this first week but talk to me), bought all my books, and finished half my semester's reading before my first class started.

Again, this is before I knew I was using any sort of productivity tricks, I just really enjoyed getting stuff done.

And so by mid-semester, about the time when most of the student body was in tears over their homework, I was having trouble finding anyone who had time to watch a movie or even order a pizza. So I found new friends at the library, friends like Ray Bradbury and Arthur C. Clarke.

They were good to me, and we remain friends to this day.

(I also have REAL friends, thanks very much for your concern.)

—

Being a Natural-Born Doer, it only became clear to me later in life that not everyone knows how to get things done. As stated in the warning section, AND the mandatory prerequisites section, most of this book assumes that you already know how to get yourself off the couch and knock things off a list.

Maybe not "finish all of your homework months ahead of time" levels of productivity, but just "do most of it on time" kind of productivity.

Conversely, if doing homework or a job assignment makes you feel weepy and usually only gets accomplished at the 11th hour, you have problems that this book probably isn't going to fix.

HOWEVER...it would be lame of me to not at least give you a bit of a shove in the right direction before jumping into the advanced stuff. I recognize that some of you will, despite all of my repeated warnings, read on without the required elementary skills.

So before we go any further, we'll look at some basic skills, and hopefully that will catch you up if need be. If you're already a doer or have already read any other productivity book, you can probably skip this section.

| BASIC SKILLS REVIEW

I'm not going to spend a lot of time on these because you're already supposed to know this stuff, but here you go:

1. Start Lifting Weights - Weight training (or resistance training) is unbelievably useful in improving your ability to get things done and feel good about it. I know that it seems like a weird thing to emphasize first, but it's huge. Benefits include:

- Improved testosterone production: This will make you FEEL more like working on tasks and more confident in your ability to accomplish them (true for both sexes, this isn't just a guy-thing).

- Improved mood: This will help prevent depression-related inactivity (sad-laziness, which is kind of like sad-eating but without the ice cream).

- Improved self-conception: I've read that studies have shown that lifting heavy weights for just a couple of reps wildly increases your self-confidence and self-perception in terms of what you believe you are "able" to do in life. I haven't bothered to verify this study or footnote it here, but as an avid weightlifter myself I can tell you that it's 100% true.

You can cite me.

- Improved discipline: Pushing through the pain of weight training in turn trains your mind to "man-up" (or woman-up) and just get stuff done.

There are obviously also other health benefits to exercising, but in accord with our subject, weight lifting is going to help train you to get things done. You can even do it at home if you get some weights and / or resistance bands (my new favorite).

*I should also note that when I started lifting weights I stopped getting sick in the winter and started needing an hour less of sleep at night, thereby gaining me a whole extra hour of time each day to get stuff done, priceless.

**I should ALSO say that you should always consult your doctor before starting a new exercise routine, I'm not a doctor, these statements are not approved by the FDA, etc., etc.

Don't hurt yourself and sue me.

2. Write It Down - You should start each day by writing down what you hope to accomplish, like your top three items, and then put them somewhere you can see them throughout the day. Why? You're something like 50% more likely to do a thing if you actually take the time to think about it clearly, and 90% more likely to do it if you take the time to write it down. And then you're like 99% more likely to follow through if you then review what you wrote down every day, morning and night. Again, no footnote, just repeating what you would have read if you went out and bought one of those "regular" productivity books like you were supposed to have done by now. I'm sure they have lots of footnotes.

How nice for you.

3. Get Accountability - You're more likely to do stuff if you know someone is going to ask you about it later.

Set up a morning / evening call with an accountability partner.

4. Set up a Public Reward / Consequence - You're also a zillion times more likely to do stuff if you know that something good / bad will happen if you do / don't accomplish it. I find rewards work better, even if it's just getting to read the news in the morning with my coffee after first accomplishing a few things I'm less naturally drawn to doing.

5. Start Your Day out with Small Wins - This is commonly expressed as "Make Your Bed". The idea is that taking control of the state of your bedroom first thing in the morning will lead to other positive, larger accomplishments throughout the day and / or relieve you of the feeling of something undone back home. Nailing a few wins early (such as brushing your teeth and making your bed) is going to be good for everyone (if only to remove the drag of being a slob on your psyche) but it does play itself out a bit differently depending on your personality:

INTROVERTS: Indispensable for task-oriented Introverts. I have a series of about a dozen small wins that I snag each morning (including making my bed) that help launch me into mid-sized tasks which, when completed, then slingshot me the energy and momentum needed to take on the largest and most difficult tasks of my day. Small wins make my life happen.

EXTROVERTS: For people-oriented Extroverts the process is going to look a bit different, and probably need to involve social accountability (see numbers 3 & 4 above) as well as incentives like meeting up with other extroverted people to do tasks together. Hard for me to visualize what this is like but I imagine it could be like a scheduled Skype first thing in the morning with your task-accountability-partner where you take 5-10 minutes to each review your to-do list to each other through the screen. But everyone is different, think about what makes you excited to do work and feel energized, and then find little ways to build that into the first part of your day.

If you don't know if you're Introverted or Extroverted you should probably figure that out.

6. Lie to Yourself - Tell yourself that you'll just "start" on writing that paper, or chapter, or project. You'll just "start" the dishes, you'll just "start" cleaning up the house. Don't set an end time, just start. And maybe part way through the job you'll say to yourself, "Hm, that looks pretty good. I'll just write one more paragraph. And just one more, and just one more...and maybe a bit more...and wait I'm done. Well...I'll just *start* the next chapter..." I do this ALL THE TIME and it's AMAZING for getting stuff done.

I'm doing it RIGHT NOW as I write this.

7. Rotate Tasks - Switching back and forth between different types of activities gives your brain the *illusion of quitting* when really you're just starting a new project. Holds true even when you "quit" the "new" project and go back to the "old" one.

8. Be Cold - Cold exposure is one of the easiest things you can do to raise your mood and energy levels on a daily basis.

Start out by ending your showers with a blast of cold water for as long as you can tolerate it. Work your way up, just be careful to take it step by step. If you go too quickly, you could black out and hit your head and die. You probably shouldn't do this if you are pregnant or have a heart condition. Always consult your doctor before experimenting with major temperature swings. Cold plunges and rolling in the snow are more advanced techniques. I do a cold plunge any chance I get, and do a cold finish on my shower every morning.

It's like an extra cup of coffee.

9. Be Organized - The silent partner of production is organization. If you are disorganized you will be unable to maintain even basic levels of productivity, or capture the value of your work. Put this book down and go read an organizational skills book.

10. Use Technology - We live in an amazing age of technological aids. There is not one perfect app for everyone, the trick is to find the 2-3 that work really well for you and then stick with them. I use Trello for task management, the labeling system in Gmail, Google docs and sheets, and Google calendar (synced up with my wife's).

11. Buy a Filing Box - Much of the world (government, banks, etc.) still uses paper. You're going to handle hundreds of thousands of pages (or in the case of business folk like myself, probably tens of millions) in your lifetime. You better have a system for filing your bills and statements and letters or you'll waste time looking for them and / or fail to act on items in a timely manner, which will create MORE work and further limit your ability to get basic things done.

Start small: Get a file box, label some folders with a sorting system that makes sense, and *use* it. I like to stack things in a little "to file" pile on my desk so I'm not filing every five minutes, and then once or twice a week, I quickly sort them into their respective files (see "Batch your Tasks" below). I have only lost / been unable to find ONE important document in the last seven years using this system, huge savings in time wasted looking for things.

Review / reset your filling system annually.

12. Batch your Tasks - Batching is doing things only once or twice a day / week / month / year instead of doing them all the time. Most people find this most helpful with regard to email. Do you need to check your email 1,700 times a day? No you do not. You can safely boil that down to 1-3 set times in your day. You can also batch return phone calls, update your calendar or to-do lists, etc. Almost anything is "batchable".

13. Isolate Your Mind - The holy grail of productivity is usually referred to as "Achieving a State of Flow", a mental framework where results simply "flow" out of you, presumably because you have managed to cut off all other non-essential brain processes and are thereby using all available resources to produce brilliant and speedy work. There are differing theories on how best to enter into a state of flow but one of the most common tricks is to throw on some headphones and listen to the same song or short playlist of songs over and over again. It may sound a little crazy but give it a try, it can be awesome.

Others would also put forth mindfulness meditation practices, but I find it easier to just hit up some Metallica.

—

I could keep going, but that's enough to get you started. If you've never heard of these before then probably you should just focus on this section for a while until you achieve a basic level of productivity / organization. Get to where you feel positive and strong.

You'll need that stability and conditioning for the advanced stuff...

| ACTION STEPS

Add one or more of these items to your morning routine (and approximate time-cost to do so):

1. Make your bed (2 minutes).

2. Do as many pushups as you can comfortably do without hurting yourself (1 minute).

3. End your shower with a blast of cold (or cool) water (10 seconds).*

4. <u>Hand-write</u> the top 3 items to accomplish that day and post it where you can see it (5 minutes).

*Again, consult your doctor before doing exercise or cold exposure; don't do it if you have physical health issues that prevent you from trying these things safely, etc.

The beginning is the most important part of the work.

- Plato

Hack #1

The 80 / 20 Principle

IT'S 2011 AND I'M at the bookstore, standing in one of the aisles, reading the "Four Hour Work Week" by Tim Ferriss for the first time. I'm not actually shopping, I'm just on a date with my wife looking at books for fun (we're weird like that) and I had heard about the FHWW and wanted to check it out for myself.

After a bit of searching I find its brightly colored spine and crack it open.

About 20% of the way into the book I feel like I have grasped about 80% of the key principles and so I put it back on the shelf and walk away, INTJ gears turning. Just glancing at those pages explained so much of the way that my brain is wired, gave me the vocabulary to talk about it, and even the tools to do some rewiring.

Remember the *gas on the fire* I talked about in the introduction? This is where it started, standing in that bookstore, clutching that unpurchased book. (I did buy a copy years later, the expanded one, as well as all Ferriss' other books and highly recommend them, but at the time that first 20% of the FHWW was all that I needed or could handle really. Also his podcast is pretty amazing, I recommend giving it a try also.)

Two principles in particular stood out to me in those pages:

1. The 80 / 20 Principle

2. Parkinson's Law

I'm going to address the 80 / 20 Principle in this chapter, and then Parkinson's Law in the next chapter.

Again, these aren't my innovations, you'll find them everywhere productivity is discussed, but they're necessary to know and so I can't skip them. You can think of them as the 201 class-level things that you need to learn before we get into the extra-advanced stuff.

First, the 80 / 20 Principle...

| HACK #1 – THE 80 / 20 PRINCIPLE

The 80 / 20 Principle is the idea that you get about 80% of the results on any given task from only the initial 20% of your time and effort put into it. Conversely, if you insist on pressing for 100% of the results, you'll spend approximately another 80% of the amount of time and energy in pursuit of that missing 20%.

*I should note that there is actually a book called "The 80 / 20 Principle" by Richard Kosh, who helped popularize the concept, which was originally put forth by an Italian economist, though he called it the "Law of Unequal Returns" or something like that. Anyway, that's probably where Ferriss picked up the concept (and he probably footnoted it?) but I haven't read the original book yet, I only recently ran across it at an airport bookstore. For now I'm avoiding reading it so that I don't accidentally trigger a new acceleration of my productivity.

I've just managed to find the sweet spot and don't want to mess things up.

Anyway, here's how this works:

| EXAMPLE – ASSIGNED PAPER

Let's say your task is to write a paper for a class you're in, and it takes you about an hour to write a paper that you know will earn you a B- grade, which in most North American schools is a mark of about an 80% (out of 100% possible). If you want to press on for an A+ grade (a score of 100%) you're going to have to spend approximately another *four hours* to get to that top-top level. But then you're going to be up until 2 am and you're only going to have time to work on that *one* paper and not accomplish anything else in that five-hour time block. And perhaps that means completely ignoring four other papers that are also due the following morning.

If instead you chose to accept a B- grade on your initial paper (80% results on the initial 20% of effort) you'd potentially have four more hours to devote to writing four other B- minus papers.

So, if you actually have five papers due, that's either one A+ (and four "incompletes") or finishing all five papers on-time and at a B- level. Unless you've got a personality (or parents) that demand straight A's on your work, most people would probably prefer a B- paper to a mark of incomplete.

By applying the 80 / 20 Principle, you can either accomplish 100% of one task, or 80% of five tasks, in the same amount of time.

The choice is between one at 100% or five at 80%.

Let's look at the Math on that...

| MATH TIME - 4X

100% results x 1 = 100% results

80% results x 5 = 400% results

The 80 / 20 Principle gives you approximately a 4x return in your productivity.

Now, you may say that you HAVE to get A+ papers or otherwise your GPA (and parents) will notice, and that's true. I only use that illustration because I find it helpful in that almost everyone has had to write a graded paper in their life at some point, so they pretty quickly grasp the numbers that are involved.

But when you grow up and enter the real world, most of your work ISN'T going to be graded in that same way. Turning in B- work is actually pretty great by professional standards, which is maybe a bit sad but totally true. People are wicked-lazy and entitled these days and often turn in pretty crappy work.

Consider also that many employers are paying by the hour and would probably greatly appreciate a 4x bump in your productivity and NOT EVEN NOTICE or CARE about the B-level quality of your work. Again, that's about the best they can expect from you anyway, and might even reflect some kind of improvement. Very few professions consistently require A+ level work, and you have to factor in that few people other than yourself are going to be as knowledgeable and critical of your work as to actually assess it as being a B- level.

Most are going to look at B- work and see A- work, simply due to their more removed vantage point.

—

*From this point on, each chapter will have a "Math Time" section, numerically representing an approximation of the potential value of each hack on your overall productivity. I include these because:

1. Some people like numbers.

2. I feel somewhat obligated to provide a measure of proof for the "ridiculous" 1,000x claim made in the subtitle.

However:

1. You might not be one of those people who likes numbers.

2. You might not care about the claim made in the title.

If that's you, then it's totally cool to skim / skip these "Math Time" sections, they aren't 100% necessary.

YOU: "Whew...I didn't want to say anything, but math just isn't my thing..."

It's OK, I don't like math very much either.

| IMPORTANT NOTE

Some people (rocket scientists, surgeons, civil engineers, your defense lawyer) need to consistently turn in A+ work because if they don't, bad things can happen (explosions, wrong-sided amputations, crumbling bridges, life in prison, etc.). So obviously this principle has to be applied within fields and situations that require less precision.

Some things shouldn't be rushed.

But for most situations, this one hack can be life-altering.

—

Got the 80 / 20 Principle down? You need to get this because a lot of what follows rides on your comprehension and appreciation of this foundational concept.

But the next one is almost equally as important...

—

| ACTION STEP*

What is one task or project that you can immediately apply the 80 / 20 Principle to?

*From this point on, instead of spreading out your energy across multiple actions steps, I'll follow up each chapter with just one (maybe two) to focus on. Usually only about 20% of end-of-chapter actions steps are actually useful anyway, I'm saving you from having to look at the other 80%.

The ultimate inspiration is the deadline.

- Nolan Bushnell

Hack #2

Parkinson's Law

It's 2002 and I'm about to candidate for my first salaried position out of college. I got a call from a board member late Thursday evening telling me that they like me but want more face time, and so they've planned out a Friday / Saturday / Sunday schedule for me to have meetings with the board, the members, and the staff. He also mentions in an off-handed manner that I could, perhaps, bring a few samples of past work.

At this point in my life I'm finished college, newly married, pushing shopping carts for Costco twenty-five hours a week, and living in a subsidized housing apartment complex that smells like garbage and curry. My wife has complained that there is only a single window to look out of and that I won't let her go outside alone because it's too dangerous (it was). The only way I am able to appease her is with individual ten cent Gerber daisies that I buy on my way home from work from a local producer, but not every day because we're too poor.

I really want this new job.

Despite the fact that I have no adequate samples ready and, due to a full shift at Costco the next day, have no time to prepare anything before the Friday evening meeting with the executive board, I say, "Sure! No problem, I'll be there with *samples*."

By 11:00 PM that same night, I'm at a Kinko's copy shop with my young bride, running photocopies and putting together portfolios of two studies / presentations that I wrote in the couple of hours that elapsed since the phone call, as well as mock ups for event flyers and a few other materials. It's literally the 11th hour as we do this. I dig out cassette tapes of me presenting material to groups in the past from my time as an intern during college. I put all of this together and go to bed very late.

The next evening, less than 24 hours from receiving the initial call, I'm passing out glossy stacks of work to the board members sitting around the table.

I get that job and work at it for the next eight and a half years.

The 2.5x increase in pay meant our new apartment had more than one window, didn't smell like curry, and I could buy my wife more than one flower at a time.

About a year later, we bought our first house and then a few years following that we flipped it two weeks before the 2008 housing crash, moving back into a rental and pocketing the gains, which we later invested in a good computer, which helped allow us to (eventually) build the thriving e-commerce business we have today.

Staying up late that night to make those portfolios? Priceless.

—

Deadlines are everything, and though I didn't know it at the time, I was obeying something called Parkinson's Law.

| HACK #2 - PARKINSON'S LAW

Parkinson's Law states that "Work expands so as to fill the time available for its completion."

I set myself a deadline of about four hours to generate and collate those portfolios (all-new content, approximately 70 minutes of presentation material) as well as all the related promotional material, handouts, etc. And in the end, that was enough time to do a good enough job at it. In other circumstances (and for many of the years that would follow at that job) I would have taken a week to generate that same amount of material, mixed in with the rest of my work and life. But because I had a firm and immediate deadline ("I can't go to bed until this is finished") I was able to accomplish the task in what was probably the very minimum amount of time that it could have taken.

All of us have experienced this, even if we haven't recognized it as taking place. Some of you actually ONLY work in the 11th hour, compressing your work into the final moments where the impending deadline *forces* you to do the work you have avoided up until this point. It's a horrible, stressful way to accomplish things, but it works.

If that's you, you're using Parkinson's Law all the time, though with little real benefit to yourself.

The beautiful thing about Parkinson's Law is that it still works even when *the deadline is artificially imposed ahead of the true due-date.* Meaning you don't have to wait until the actual, real-world deadline to force yourself to do stuff.

We'll look at a couple of examples, one where you've got an Externally Imposed Deadline somewhere in the near future, but you'd like to bring that deadline closer to finish the work earlier, and then another situation where there really isn't any real deadline at all, and it's up to you to make up an Internally Imposed Deadline for yourself.

First let's look at the more traditional situation: you've got something with an Externally Imposed Deadline…

| EXAMPLE #1 - EXTERNALLY IMPOSED DEADLINE

Back to grade school again: Let's say you've got a project due, and the teacher has pegged the due date as being in 30 days from now.

Parkinson's Law says that if you give yourself a month to finish that project, it's going to take you a month to finish it.

However! The power in Parkinson's Law is that the following is ALSO true:

If you give yourself until the next morning to finish that project, you're probably going to have it finished by the morning, even if you have to stay up all night and ask your mom for help, you're going to have SOMETHING ready to take to school with you in the morning.

Is staying up all night to get the work done 29 days early hard? Yes. And feel unnecessary? Probably. But what feels better, 29 days of stressing a project that you just can't seem to start, or 29 days of knowing it's finished and being able to move on with your life?

If you pay the price, the freedom is worth it.

Now you don't actually have to stay up late a month ahead of time to finish a school project, but you CAN use that kind of intense artificial time-restriction to "Red Button" yourself into getting a huge amount of work done in a small amount of time. And in a world of externally imposed deadlines, that's an important skill to have.

But what if you have something you'd simply *like* to do but there isn't anyone out there externally imposing a due-date?...

| EXAMPLE #2 - INTERNALLY IMPOSED DEADLINE

Say you have a self-imposed goal such as writing a book. It's pretty nebulous, there isn't any sort of external force applying itself to you or your goal (no agent or publisher breathing down your neck because you received a $100,000 book advance and ran off to Mexico and blew it on Tequila).

So it's 100% up to you to set a deadline for yourself.

Parkinson's Law says that:

1. If you don't set a firm deadline, you will NEVER finish your book.

2. If you set a deadline of three years from now, it will take you three years (at least) to write your book, if ever you finish it at all (a deadline set far enough out in the future has about the same effect of not setting one at all, see point #1 above).

3. However if you give yourself two weeks to write your book, you will probably have SOMETHING to show for it by the end of the two weeks, even if it sucks and isn't really polished enough to publish at that point. (There is a certain amount of "lying to yourself" that can be helpful in setting extremely short deadlines, see Basic Skill #5).

I managed to write the first draft of this book in just three days over a Christmas holiday break. Was it ready to publish? Not even close, but because I gave myself just a few days to "finish" it, I completed more than I could have dreamed even if I had given myself six months.

—

How does Parkinson's Law stack up against the 80 / 20 Principle in terms of multiplying your productivity? Let's do some math...

| MATH TIME - 6X

Compared with the 80 / 20 Principle, it's a little more work to quantify the *numerical* value of Parkinson's Law, but it can be done.

First let's start with a given of the set amount of hours in a day: 24. The first place that Parkinson's Law begins to capture value is by stealing new hours out of your day that would have otherwise been dedicated to other things, things such as Facebook, eating, talking on the phone, watching TV, sleeping, etc. There is an enormous amount of fluff in each of our daily lives, stuff that we don't HAVE to do (social media, watching tv, phone calls) and other things that can, for the most part, be safely postponed or shortened (eating, sleeping).

Is it sustainable to perpetually "rob Peter to pay Paul" in this way? Can you ignore your friends, food, and rest for weeks on-end? No you can't, and that's OK, because this book isn't about helping you be productive on a daily, normal basis.

It's about how to go into "emergency mode" and temporarily move mountains.

(No one moves mountains every day and lives to tell about it.)

So the first bit of math we get to do is estimate (very approximately) the power of cutting the fluff from your life to focus on your project.

Let's say that this project is within the scope of doing your job or workday, and that normally you work 8-10 hour days. It is reasonable to suggest that you could double the amount of time you spent on a project to 16-20 hours, and not die.

Some of those hours your mind might begin to falter and fail to give good quality work, but with some breaks, naps, and coffee, you could probably do it.

This is also proportionally true if you are tackling a project that is outside of your daily work, such as night school, or even a side project at work that can only be done AFTER you've fulfilled your 8 hours of regular duties in the office and then commuted home, etc. Let's say that you were thinking of spending 3-4 hours on the project in the evening, but instead "pulled an all-nighter" and stayed up late to do 6-8 hours of work on it. You had just enough time to get a few hours of sleep and then back to class, or work, or whatever you do with your day.

In EITHER CASE, you're seeing an obvious 2x of your productivity, simply based on the amount of time you're spending on it. But there is also a HIDDEN productivity boost in that with the imposed "next day" type of deadline, out of desperation you also cut out all of the interruptions that normally would occur. You turn off your phone, and kill all of your other browser tabs, lock the doors and pull down the shades, wear headphones, drink an energy drink and KNUCKLE DOWN way beyond what you would normally do.

Why does this matter? How does focusing and cutting out interruptions and distractions affect our productivity?

Studies have shown that for every interruption while working (notification ping, phone call, Steve from accounting, etc.) it takes us about 25 minutes to fully refocus on the task at hand. If you average 2-3 interruptions an hour, you are literally NEVER WORKING AT FULL CAPACITY.

So the other numerically quantifiable benefit of Parkinson's Law is that when you isolate yourself in every way possible to focus as deeply as is possible for the longest period of time, you become 3-4x more productive. No footnote here, no study to back this up, so maybe don't quote this section's math, but using common sense: If you are regularly allowing for interruptions to your work day, cutting those out is going to allow you to get 3-4 times as much stuff done.

Anyone who has tried isolation can vouch for those kinds of numbers. It won't be a lot more than that, nor a lot less.

Taken TOGETHER, the 2x value of the capture of "fluff time" out of your day, and the potential 4x value of capturing lost attention and focus, the total potential value of applying an artificial deadline to your work is about 6x. This is even slightly greater of an effect than is available with the 80 / 20 Principle, though less sustainable / applicable over the long run.

| IMPORTANT NOTE

Just by itself, Parkinson's Law is incredibly powerful, but only when used realistically. If you're prone to discouragement because you feel like you failed to finish on time, over-using this "Law" might end up putting you into a downward spiral. You might get depressed and lose momentum if all you manage to do is set up a series of "missed deadlines".

Make up deadlines that are <u>realistic</u> and that are most likely to set you up for the nearest-reachable win.

—

Are the 80 / 20 Principle and Parkinson's Law lodged in your brain? Ready to go deeper?

Now let's get crazy.

| ACTION STEP

What project do you have hanging over you right now that you can finish by Midnight tonight?

A year from now you may wish you had started today.

- Karen Lamb

Hack #3

Parkinson's 20

It's 2013 and I'm cutting myself off from the world to write for two weeks. I've decided to start a blog and I am determined to avoid the fate of most blogs, which I'm sure you've seen before:

The grand initial post, announcing the majesty of the blog to come: the posts, the laughs, the greatness, the multitude of written words (you know what I'm talking about) and then:

NOTHING.

#bloggerfail

So many bloggers announce their intentions to the world (which is a dangerous thing to do by the way, robs you of much of the energy to actually DO the thing, that could be Basic Skill #14) and then totally fail to follow through with any of it. MAYBE they write one more post, maybe two, but then nothing else, forever.

Determined that this wouldn't be me, I set out to pre-write a year of weekly blog posts, 52 in all.

Ahead of time.

That way I couldn't fail, right? Not if they were already written.

It was a lofty goal for sure, but it was one I *accomplished*. How? By doing it *faster*.

Obviously I started out by using Parkinson's Law to give myself a *constrained* amount of time to write the 52 posts. That's 52 posts in 14 days, meaning I'd have to write 3 or 4 posts a day to hit the magic 52. All well and good to say, but how do you possibly maintain that level of intensity and actually pull off that mountain of work? By boiling that work down to only the most important 20% that would deliver the most important 80% of the material within the constraint of two weeks.

I used the 80 / 20 principle AND Parkinson's rule *together*, something I call Parkinson's 20.

| HACK #3 - PARKINSON'S 20

I know what you're thinking:

"Hey! You just combined the two principles together to make up a new principle!"

Yes I did, and it's the first step to maximizing what each of these principles can do for us. It's all well and good if you spend only 14 days on a project instead of 365, using Parkinson's Law to limit the overall time-frame that you have for a task or project and forcing you to steal time from other activities, cut yourself off from distractions, etc., but you can and should also maximize the benefits of the 80 / 20 Principle when working with a limited time-frame.

Together these principles take your productivity to a whole new level.

Let's look at an example...

| EXAMPLE - YEAR OF BLOG POSTS

If we use my example of starting a weekly blog, let's say that would normally be two hours of writing per post, from story idea to final draft, with the goal of generating 52 posts over the course of a year, which would total about 104 hours of work.

By applying Parkinson's Law, I could give myself two weeks to FORCE myself to produce 52 blog posts, do the 104 hours in two week's time. That's 52 hours a week, or about 10.4 hours a day, five days a week, for two consecutive weeks (and weekends off).

Would I be more likely to get all those posts written within a YEAR if I first tried to write them all in just TWO WEEKS? For sure. But, as we looked at in the last chapter, Parkinson's

Law has certain limitations over the long term, two weeks is a long time to ignore your family and spend all your time hunched over a keyboard. You will probably go crazy and eventually find yourself standing on a bridge, contemplating the importance of blogging in the larger scheme of things (an enormously valid question to be asking yourself).

HOWEVER, if you also apply the 80 / 20 Principle to that 104 hours of work, you might accept 80% of the most significant results in just 20.8 hours, saving 83.2 hours of work. That boils down to just over two hours a day of hyper-focused work, which is the difference between you getting your blog written and standing on that bridge.

Now you might say, "That's easy to SAY that you can get 80% of the results out of just 20% of the effort, but writing and typing take actual TIME."

And you would be right, so I will go an extra step here and give you EXACTLY what that looked like for me so you can imagine how it might work in other real-world situations:

In terms of me writing blog posts in the real world, using Parkinson's 20 meant grinding out the longest rough draft I could, polishing it once, all in the time allotted (about 24 minutes), and then doing another. Or in some cases, writing a different draft before going back to polish the first (task-switching, Basic Skill #7), and lying to myself the whole time that I could stop anytime I want (Basic Skill #6). This, along with isolating myself and telling my community to leave me alone for two weeks, allowed me to accomplish my goal.

To be completely honest, my posts weren't perfect, but when it came time to actually put them up live on the blog each week, they only needed the quickest polish before they were ready to go, and in the end, that's what made doing the blog possible. The hard part was over, only the fun part was left.

When using Parkinson's Law to set artificial limits on your project, first applying the 80 / 20 Principle to boil down to the most important elements of your task is not only a huge time savings, it can also help prevent your general use of Parkinson's Law from being an exercise in frustration. *Without* also using the 80 / 20 Principle, you may flail about trying to get a bunch of stuff "done" in the shorter time frame but end up with nothing but straw for your efforts because you didn't know what to focus on.

How does this work out in terms of real productivity increases? Math time...

| MATH TIME - 10X

Again, anytime you mix in Parkinson's Law, the math is less concrete, but essentially you can think of it in terms of adding together previously figured values of the 80 / 20 Principle (4x) and Parkinson's Law (6x).

Doing so we can estimate that Parkinson's 20 pushes your *potential* overall productivity to a nice rounded 10x.

10x in productivity means Parkinson's 20 could boil 100 hours of work down into just 10 hours.*

*Again, this is only approximately what is achievable. How much of an increase you'd see over your usual productivity is largely based on how much you previously tended to procrastinate. If you were already loath to wait to finish a project, you're going to see much less of an x return using this principle (closer to the original 4x that the plain 80 / 20 is going to achieve for you) but that's only true because in a way you were ALREADY using the P-Law to get yourself into gear and finish up your projects early (which was my experience).

However even if this is just giving a name to what you already do, being more self-aware will allow you to be that much more intentional about it.

| IMPORTANT NOTE

It's probably a good idea at this moment to point out that these two principles (and their combined form) only work on some *kinds* of work. If you think about it, most work would fall into one of four major categories:

Producing Something (e.g., writing material)

Consuming Something (e.g., reading material)

Face-time with Humans (e.g., work meetings)

Problem Solving (e.g., math work)

These principles work really well on the first two categories of work, producing and consuming.

They are less effective when you have to give actual face-time with humans, at meetings and whatnot, though if you are setting the agenda you can often speed things up by setting a firm end-time and focusing on only the most important 20% of topics, etc. You can also speed things up by setting artificial time constraints (my parking meter is ending) and by choosing isolating environments to conduct meetings (outdoors in winter).

Problem solving is the one area of work that you're unable to push much faster using these principles. Focusing on the most important elements of a problem can help you suss out the solution faster, as well as staying up late and isolating yourself, but the brain drain of these types of hacks will quickly start to work against you.

Instead, consider that if you apply these hacks in all the other areas of your life you'll end up with more time to freely focus on those problem solving types of jobs, and at least end up with a *net* productivity gain.

—

Now at this point you may say, "Look, I can't do 80 hours of work in just 8 hours, that's impossible."

And yeah, again, maybe that's true for you. If you're a rocket scientist, or a surgeon, or a civil engineer...some people can't rush their work and / or accept less than 100% perfection.

But for most people, the only reason it takes them so long to get stuff done is because they they are just giving themselves TOO MUCH TIME to overthink it and then pressing for an EXCELLENCE THAT DOESN'T MATTER to anyone and that no one will probably even notice or care about in the end.

So if you're not a Rocket Surgeon then maybe you can safely use Parkinson's 20 to 10x your productivity, at least in temporary situations, when the need arises.

And perhaps you should just be happy with that, 10x is pretty good, most productivity books leave it at that...maybe this is as far as you want to read?

Because things get a little hardcore from this point on...

—

| ACTION STEP

What project do you have hanging over you right now that you can finish the most important 20% of within the next hour?

Put this book down and get started right now.

There is nothing impossible to him who will try.

- Alexander the Great

Hack #4

20 of 20

IT'S 2015 AND I'M attempting to learn how to use the program Scrivener by reading through the instruction PDF, which is horribly long and not really my thing. Normally I just try and USE a program and then figure it out as I go along, but this time I'm thinking that I should probably actually make an attempt to read the manual, just so I don't screw things up and waste time.

That said, I CANNOT bring myself to read the whole thing, and instead start looking for how I can just read the most important 20%. And then, "What's this?? They've already created a shorter version of the instructions with only the MOST IMPORTANT information? They've already identified my 20% for me!!"

Five minutes later my eyes are glazed over as I attempt to read the "shortened" version of the instructions.

Automatically my mind begins to look for the most important 20% of this new 20%, skims through and finds it, and learns

Scrivener in record time. Do I know how to use every little feature? Far from it. Am I using it successfully right at this moment to craft this book?

Yes I am.

It was only later, after reflecting on what took place that day, that I began thinking about what I had done, and the implications it had raised:

What if you applied the 80 / 20 Principle TO the 80 / 20 Principle?...would the same math hold up?

It does.

I call it 20 of 20.

| HACK #4 – 20 OF 20

The 80 / 20 Principle is all about finding the most important 20%, the part of the work / task / job that is most central and gives those 80% of the results. Sometimes that's just putting pen to paper, or getting something major moved from one place to the next, just getting it done, right? It's that first 20% that really matters.

BUT, I found that inside that initial 20% is ANOTHER 20%, the 20 of the 20 that is the most-most important, and if you get *that* 20% done (which is only 4% of the original) you'll STILL have 64% of the results (using just 20% of the most important 20%).

Did you follow that?

Let's look at an example...

| EXAMPLE - DEPARTMENT REVIEW

Suppose you're the head of a corporate division of the company you work for and your boss asks you for a full department review. You could immediately launch into a series of interviews with all of your staff, ask for written and oral updates on all of their various projects, hit up accounting for the freshest numbers, sit down with HR and ask about what kind of interpersonal issues are currently at play, recommendations, etc. You could run around all week and spend 50 hours gathering info and then another 10 hours over the weekend drafting it all into a written report, synthesizing the information into trends, problems, potential solutions, etc.

Would you get an A+ for effort? Would your boss be impressed? Probably yes on both counts.

But at what cost? You stirred up your whole team for a week just to write a paper that your boss will only read (skim?) once and retain only the 4% that he really cares the most about. Which then begs the question - *What is that 4%?* Perhaps it's the part that is most central to the core mission of the business, or maybe it's a personal beef he has with another top level exec that he needs to prove wrong on a particular point, or maybe he just needed it to hand something to HIS boss.

And maybe his boss doesn't care about anything except the current trend of the company share price.

What if that was the case and you *knew that ahead of time?*

What if you just asked your boss a few questions about the final destination of the report, and if there are any key data-points that he's especially interested to have. If you can nail down that 4% target ahead of time, you'll be able to drill down on that in just one or two workdays and have it back on his desk before the weekend.

YOU: "But if I just give him 4% of a report, won't he freak out? Won't he see that as wildly unfinished?"

Not if it's the right 4%.

YOU: "Still..."

I know, math is hard. Let me lay it out again step by step, this is literally how it works out:

| MATH TIME - 20X

100% effort = 100% results

20% effort = 80% results

4% effort = 64% results

I know what you're thinking now, "What if we do it *AGAIN*??" Well you can, and initially it looks amazing:

1% effort = 51.2% results

But reality is that on a letter grade scale, that's a D- minus. Your boss or whomever is going to notice that. You probably need to stick to aiming for the 60-80% range of results, meaning you're going to produce C- to B- level work. And to hit that you probably need to be sticking to the 4-20% range of effort. Go any deeper and I think that the math starts to fail in most real-world examples.

(**NOTE** - Despite my example above, you usually cannot just look for the "most important 4%", you need to go through the process of boiling it down to 20%, and then boiling *that* down to 20%. That's the only way it works that would result in you getting the right 4%. This is also a bit of a psychological trick because looking for the most important 4% straight away is mentally taxing.)

—

YOU: "Wait, won't my boss / partner / client notice if I'm turning in work that is less than "A" quality? Won't that be a problem?"

Yes, IF you apply this principle indiscriminately. Remember that these principles can be dangerous if not carefully handled. The 20 of 20 hack is primarily to help you avoid being the person who focuses so much on perfecting the *one* task, that they fail to do the whole of their job in a reasonable period of time. Knowing when to bring your "A" game and when to just "get it done" is an important task-sorting skill, and when applied correctly, ultimately frees you up to do your very best work on the very few tasks that actually demand it (more on this in chapter 8).

YOU: "Yeah but C level work is never going to be OK, on any of my tasks..."

Remember that perfection is in the eye of the beholder, and that anything you see up close as being C- or B- level work is going to jump a letter grade in the eyes of most other people, IF it's an area that they see as secondary to their primary focuses. When working in an environment with other people (as opposed to being a "solopreneur" or self-employed) it's key to learn to align yourself with the tasks that are centrally important so that they get your best, and to use 20 of 20 to blast through the secondary items and necessary evils (like email, billing, etc.).

—

Back to our example, that might look like finding out which 20% your boss cares about and then using the 80 / 20 Principle in producing the most important 20% of he wants (which is only 4% of your original work target but will generate 64% of what he REALLY wants, in the midst of what physically appears to be a 90-100% complete report).

But perhaps more significant: With 20 of 20, you're doing better than 4x'ing your productivity (like you would get with just 80 / 20). If you get down below the most important 20% and can hover between 4% and 20% on your work, you are also potentially pushing your productivity WAY up:

Normal 80 / 20 Principle = 4x Productivity (Remember - 80% of results X 5 = 400%)

20 of 20 = 16x Productivity (So likewise: 64% of results X 25 = 1600%)

So your boss might not mind that you're sometimes turning in (what he perceives to be) only B or B+ work when you're doing 16 TIMES the amount of work that your fellow employees are.

That's the math on 20 of 20, but what about adding Parkinson's Law back into the mix? I could write a whole other chapter on this but I don't think you need me to, we'll just do the math here and then keep moving forward.

When we roll back in Parkinson's Law and apply the 80 / 20 rule to the TIME factor in terms of artificial deadline setting, we get into the 20x range.

We could call this Parkinson's 20 of 20.

| IMPORTANT NOTE

Now already 20x is a lot faster than most people should ever be doing anything.

Filing your taxes at 20x? Audit.

Dating your wife at 20x? Divorce.

Driving to work at 20x? Death.

So please try using some common sense when applying this. It's like shifting gears on a manual transmission. Can you rev the RPM's up into that little red area on the dial so as to be able to pop the clutch and start on a hill? Sure you can. Is it possible to drive at between 6000-7000 RPM's all the time and not destroy your engine?

No, it's not.

So Parkinson's 20 of 20 is best used only when you need a quick burst of speed that can be safely applied to a task that is, perhaps, standing in your way and needs to just get done NOW.

20x still not fast enough for you? Want to go FASTER?

Three more hacks to go...

—

| ACTION STEP

Pick a project you have and boil it down to the most important 20%. Now, maybe just for practice, attempt to repeat the process and boil that down to 20% to find the most important 4% of the original project total.

Attempt to do this on several different kinds of projects, tasks, and responsibilities in your life until it becomes natural. Don't always force yourself down to 20 of 20, if you can even get to 50% of the original 20%, that will already be 10% of the original 100%, and a big jump in your productivity.

Synergy: The combined effect of individuals in collaboration that exceeds the sum of their individual effects.

- Stephen Covey

Hack #5

Synergized 20

It's 2015 and I'm driving to New York State from Montreal, a trip I am making three times a week for a few months this year to bring customer orders through an informal importation process at the commercial border entry of the U.S., and then drop them off at the USPS. I'd decided to give the process a try after hearing about it at a networking event in the Montreal Shopify offices.

Given that the Canadapost light packet shipping rates had more than doubled in the last five years, I was ready to try anything.

After a gross amount of research and trial and error, I'd managed to work out the appropriate (and legal) way to fill out the paperwork and do the import / export of commercial goods. The result is that Tuesday, Thursday, and Friday I'm taking my little blue Civic through the commercial entry point in Champlain, NY.

95% of the vehicles that come through there are giant semi-trucks, so the customs guys are like twelve feet off the ground. When I pull up to the customs "window", all I see is a wall of concrete. I have to get out of my car, and surrounded by the rumble of dozens of diesel engines, stand in the frame of my door to reach up with my passport and documents. Questions are shouted down, answers are shouted up, often unreceived.

Stressful.

But eventually they get to know me as the bearded American guy in the little blue car who married a Canadian and is now running a business out of Montreal, and things settle into a nice routine. Takes up about 8-9 hours a week of my time to make these trips, depending on the wait at the border and the weather (Montreal has the same winter as Moscow = Deadly Snow).

And you might think that this whole thing is a huge pain but I'm super happy about making the trips: we're saving money on postage like crazy (enough that after a few months I'm able to pay someone else to make these trips and we're still saving overall), our customers are getting their orders faster, they finally have tracking numbers on them, and I'm getting some much needed personal time sitting in the car (working from home isn't the same as going to the office, us Introverts need our alone time).

And on top of all that, I've got my laptop open next to me and I'm making the original notes for this book via a headmic and the crappy free voice recognition software bundled into Apple's Pages software. Yes, my notes were nearly unreadable, not worth attempting to rewrite, but my ideas were captured, and this book now exists.

The point that I'd like to make with this is that in-all, I'm accomplishing at least five important objectives, all at the same time:

1. Saving money on postage

2. Providing faster shipping for our customers

3. Providing tracking information for our customers

4. Getting important personal alone time to recharge emotionally

5. Drafting notes for this book

The multifaceted nature of these trips I took last year illustrate something I call the Synergized 20.

| HACK #5 – SYNERGIZED 20

Have you ever heard the expression, killing two birds with one stone? This is a euphemism for getting two things done at the SAME TIME using the SAME EFFORT.

But why stop at two birds? What about killing five birds and wounding two others? With a single stone?

(NOTE - Throwing rocks at birds is probably considered immoral and / or illegal in your town, so don't do it.)

Synergy is when you have multiple things feeding back into one another, thereby creating a greater sum than the individual parts, like:

1 + 1 + 1 = 5

And normally the term synergizing refers to the net gain of *people* working together, the output being greater than the sum of its parts. But I've found that the same can hold true if you synergize between different TASKS, no extra people involved.

Synergizing tasks is where you end up accomplishing and / or making progress on multiple tasks with the same effort and time without obvious task-switching (which is really just multitasking).

A Synergized 20 is *synergizing the most important 20% (or 4%) of your tasks* by capturing their *overlapping and future potentials*.

YOU: "This still sounds like multitasking, and science has proven it doesn't make you faster..."

This is significantly different from multitasking, which is just rapidly switching between conscious tasks and wearing yourself out, like throwing rocks at birds *and* at the same time trying to wield a shotgun against a bear. Exhausting and dangerous; you probably won't hit any birds if you're throwing distracted and trying to hold a shotgun at the same time.

Probably all the birds will get away and the bear will eat you.

Instead I'm talking about tasks that can be done simultaneously with <u>no multitasking-friction</u>, and which can synergistically feed into each other *and* future tasks. If you can't add another layer of productive value on top of what you're already doing without actively switching your attention, then that task doesn't count, you've stepped into multitasking.

YOU: "I'm going to need an example of this."

I'll give you two, because true synergizing of tasks often ends up taking one of the two following forms, though they're not limited to this...

| EXAMPLE #1 - PRE-LEARNING

Pre-learning is choosing to engage with a topic related to both a current objective AND a future task, so that when you approach the future task with your full attention you can hit a much higher range of accomplishment with much less effort.

Let's say you're tired, need to rest, and want to watch TV. But instead of watching *Seinfeld* you watch a documentary about Bitcoins because you know that in about two years you're going to need to incorporate digital currency into your portfolio.

When the time comes for you to actually make the jump into digital currency investment, you're lightyears ahead of the next guy who is still trying to understand the Blockchain article on Wikipedia.

| EXAMPLE #2 - PRE-DOING

Another way this can work is when you're capturing the future value of your current task. I call this Pre-Doing.

Let's say you're training someone on how to make a new variant on a spreadsheet that's common to the projects your team works on, and you use QuickTime to screen capture the visual and audio of the training so that you NEVER HAVE TO TRAIN ANYONE ON THAT EVER AGAIN. Instead you just email new people a link to the video hosted on Vimeo or YouTube or whatever, and tell them to let you know if they have any questions. If it takes you 20 minutes to do the training the first time, and you end up sending out the link to the video 15 times over the course of the next few years, you've saved yourself 5 hours of future meetings.

Imagine if you found ways to do this ALL THE TIME.

—

There are other ways you can Synergize your work but they are usually variations of one or both of the above.

I rarely do things that don't have multiple future applications. Because of the way my brain is wired, I tend to have several different sized and overlapping projects going on at any given time. And that's the key term here: Overlapping

As I appear to be doing just one thing, I'm actually usually doing work that will have an effect on many different things, effectively killing several birds at the same time. If this was literal, my yard would be a mass-grave of dead songbirds, eagles, and hawks. PETA would be permanently camped outside my home, and I would probably be under federal investigation for killing spotted owls, seagulls, and maybe even a bald eagle or two.

NOTE - Pre-doing is often an important component of systemizing, something we'll look at in the next chapter.

—

Remember: multitasking is where you're trying to talk to someone on the phone and write an email at the same time. #Lame. Synergizing is where you save time on the future by dual-purposing or capturing your work now. #awesomepants

Let's look back at what I was doing on those road trips:

- Reducing Our Postage Expenses (increasing net profit)

- Reducing Shipping Times (improving customer experience)

- Making Tracking Numbers Available (improving customer experience even more)

- Getting Personal Time Alone (that otherwise would have been me sitting on the couch or some other form of unredeemed time)

- Writing Notes on this Book (and others, and / or sometimes I would study self-publishing via Podcast's, etc.)

I'm STILL reaping benefits from that synergized work, in ways that are hard to quantify. And both of the Pre-Learning & Pre-Doing examples were real-world ones from my life. This stuff really works.

What does it add to our maths? A lot...

| MATH TIME – 50X

Making the most of your time by doing more than one thing at the same time is even harder to quantify than Parkinson's Law, but if you practice it and consider it over the long-term, you can often get double or even triple the results you would see otherwise. I'm already using Parkinson's 20 of 20 to squeeze 20x the results out of 100% of my effort. With a Synergized 20 I'm doubling or tripling down on that effort to get two or three times the results, sometimes immediately, though usually only in the long run.

How does this work practically? Using the example of this book, I was able to bang out the first draft (80% of the content with 20% effort) with only about 5% of the effort because I had synergistically already worked through all of the concepts and thoughts I had and got them out onto paper as I was making those trips to NY and back.

Yes, I still had to sit down and actually write the book, but I was able to still hit 80% of the initial results with only 5% of the initial effort because of the pre-work I had bundled into my other activities that I would have done anyway, without slowing myself down on those projects (improving profits, customer experience, and my alone-time rest).

All of the numbers that we use when we talk about "productivity" are simply artificial constructions for the sake of illustration, but if we continue to imagine, what does a Synergized Parkinson's 20 of 20 look like compared with our prior systems?

Normal 80 / 20 Principle = 4x Productivity

Parkinson's 20 = 10x Productivity

20 of 20 = 16x Productivity

Parkinson's 20 of 20 = 20x Productivity

Synergizing = 2-3x

And then considering the synergizing effect over the long term, it acts as a *multiple* on the 20x of Parkinson's 20 of 20:

Synergized Parkinson's 20 of 20 = 40-60x Productivity (or an average of something like 50x)

| IMPORTANT NOTE

Now obviously we're getting up into the upper reaches of the stratosphere of ridiculous levels of productivity. Obviously it's not possible to actually, perfectly hit 50x productivity all the time, nor would you want to.

But if you could EVER hit that level even once a week, and / or be anywhere close to that on your productive multiplier...well you get the idea.

And yeah this is where the health problems start to kick in, God never intended us to be this productive. Just because you can pull off 40-60x productivity with these hacks doesn't mean that you should attempt to do this all the time or even ever. It can be habit-forming and, in my case, it took me a LONG time to deprogram myself from working this way.

Now it's only there if I need it and want to risk using it.

Also at this point you're obviously accomplishing a lot of DIFFERENT things, because you can't do more than 100% of any one project and when you're looking at 60x on 100% that's 6,000%. How do you do 6,000% of a school paper? You can't. Instead you're cranking out a dozen papers and rolling those forward into college application essays so that two years later when you apply to Yale or wherever, you've already got some good material for your portfolio.

How did you know which topics they would ask about on a Yale application two years ahead of time? You bothered to look into it on your smartphone while you were otherwise unoccupied on the school bus, and then asked your teacher if you could write on THOSE topics for your English class.

KEY LIFE SKILL - If you tell your public high school teacher you'd like to write Yale entrance essays for school credit, they will say yes.

YOU: "Hm...I don't think I would have ever thought to do that, even knowing these principles."

Oh but you will. Once your mind starts to work on problems in this way, you'll suddenly feel this yawning chasm open up in your mind where doing 50x productivity starts to be real. Staring into that void, all things will suddenly feel possible.

YOU: "Uh, chasm in the *void*? That sounds scary."

It's kind of like when that guy in Space Odyssey 2001 goes through the monolith and rapidly ages until being reborn as a timeless space-baby.

YOU: "What?"

Oh, uh, sorry, spoilers.

YOU: "This sounds more like Pandora's Box."

Ah...yes that might have been a better analogy.

YOU: "But that box is bad, why would you be teaching people to open that?"

Well it's not like I didn't *repeatedly* warn you for like the first three sections...and we're not done yet...if you're having second thoughts, maybe you should stop here? It's not too late.

YOU: "...it feels too late to turn back."

Actually yes, it is too late for you. I was lying when I said that it wasn't because I felt bad.

—

We've got two more hacks to hit and since it's already too late to go back, you might as well finish what you started...

| ACTION STEP

What are you doing this week that could be synergistically valuable down the road? How can you frictionlessly capture that value?

*Everything must be made as simple as possible.
But not simpler.*

- Albert Einstein

Hack #6

Systemized 20

It's 2017 and I'm receiving something like 100 "real" emails a day across seven different inboxes. (I have a bad habit of making up new projects that for some reason require a *new* email address, in my mind anyway.

These emails are from customers, e-commerce platforms & applications, analytic reports, colleagues, contract workers, friends, family, banks, payment systems, and my accountant. That figure *doesn't* include all of the news service subscriptions, ads, promotional emails, and spam. There are easily another 100-150 of those a day that make an effort to hide the "real" emails so that I don't see them right away.

And as you are painfully aware, email arrives constantly and relentlessly, day and night, all requiring some form of evaluation and response, and usually one that cannot be put off for very long.

And it seems to only get exponentially worse over time, despite any efforts to curb incoming mail (manically turning off notifications and hitting unsubscribe).

As a result of this deluge, email is often listed as one of the biggest sources of stress and / or unhappiness in people's modern lives. One friend I have said he simply walked away from his inbox entirely. He just gave up opening his emails, thus allowing his "unread messages" meter to balloon into a horrifying FIVE-DIGIT figure.

I got heart-palpitations just looking at a screenshot of it.

Yet despite the growing volume of email I get on a daily basis, I would say that I manage to spend less than an hour a day (on average) dealing with it. This is compared to an industry average of 3-4 hours a day in the corporate world (that's at least a THIRD of their workday, just on email!) or perhaps 2-3 hours a day for regular non-corporate folk.

The reason that it is even possible for me to boil it down to under an hour a day is partly due to delegation (which we'll get to in the next chapter) but the main reason is due to *systemization*, and specifically something I call the Systemized 20.

| HACK #6 - SYSTEMIZED 20

The Systemized 20 is where you systemize the responses to 80% of your regularly occurring or anticipated tasks so that they are more rapidly deployed and less mentally draining, and only provide innovative or custom responses to the most irregular or unanticipated 20% of incoming tasks.

That's kind of a long sentence so I'm going to say that again but break it down a bit:

The reality is that about 80% of what you do is something you've had to do before, and something you'll likely have to do again in the future. In those cases it's unnecessarily time-consuming to approach them from square-one each time they arrive (daily, monthly, annually, etc.). Instead you are MUCH better off taking a few extra minutes (or even hours) to develop some kind of systemized response or guide to enable you to blast through those tasks in the future, usually in a fraction of the time because you're not bogged down attempting to "reinvent the wheel".

Doing so allows you to spend MUCH more time on providing a creative response to the 20% of tasks that would most benefit from it (or simply cannot be systemized). Systemization frees you up to ENJOY these parts of your work because you're not so under the gun of simply trying to keep up with it all. Instead you have much more time and mental space to be able to approach the remaining 20% in an unhurried and creative way. This also means you're more likely to produce *better* work and can result in a deeper measure of personal success.

Also this is your LIFE we're talking about here, you should be aiming to try and have *some* fun along the way.

I know this is a tricky one to apply, let's look at a couple of examples to see how this plays out...

| EXAMPLE #1 - USING STANDARD RESPONSES FOR EMAIL

Back when our business really started taking off, we began getting the same (or very similar) questions from customers over and over again. Despite answering these questions in a very obvious FAQ page on our website, the questions still came. Answering all of them took hours and crafting custom responses to each email was not just time-consuming, it was also mentally draining.

But because so many of those emails were similar in nature, we found that about 80% of them could be responded to or dealt with in a systemized manner, requiring minimal time or mental energy. Very quickly we learned to use what we call "Standard Responses": we would craft the perfect reply to whatever nagging issue was repeatedly coming up (pre-doing) and then just cut and paste that in whenever the next email arrived (systemized response).

We still use this system in our business today, and we're always creating new Standard Response documents. Once we get the same question more than three times, it gets flagged for me by my team and I crank out a new standardized response which becomes available to the whole team and saves us all time.

The net result is that we cut down our response time for 80% of our emails from something like 10 minutes to 1 minute.

Let me tell you, that adds up.

But enough with email, what about something a little more complicated, maybe where you can't involve any pre-doing?...

| EXAMPLE #2 - ANNUAL FILINGS FOR A NON-PROFIT ORGANIZATION

In addition to being involved in business, I also sit on the board of a non-profit organization (our church) as the Secretary / Treasurer, and generally fulfill a volunteer executive role alongside the paid staff. A large part of my duties has been to interface with all of our legal, fiscal, and operational partners such as banks, insurance agents, accountants, landlords, payroll companies, and government agencies galore.

As you might imagine, it can get complicated.

For example, each year, nonprofits are required to file a bunch of pieces of paper with various agencies. Sometimes they need to be given to the employees, sometimes to the government, sometimes a hardcopy must be sent in the mail, sometimes submitted online electronically, sometimes the accountant is supposed to do it, and sometimes I'm supposed to.

CONFESSION: With the volume of stuff I have going on, I have trouble remembering how to do anything if more than three months have elapsed since I last did it. It just gets swept out to sea by the tide of my life.

So when stuff is *annual* in nature (such as the annual schedule of our non-profit filings) I'm always finding myself starting at zero. Not only do I have trouble remembering WHEN to do it, I'm also at a complete loss as to HOW to do it. Also I usually can't "pre-do" these type of tasks, so in order to survive and thrive in these types of situations I've had to develop and commit to a couple of systems (both of which make use of technology, see Basic Skill #10):

First, I created a spreadsheet in Google Docs where I listed out each annual item by date, name, task, responsibility (me or someone else), and any useful links / notes to help jumpstart me. I color-coded each of the lines to immediately indicate to me if it was something I was supposed to do or not, or if there was a step I was partially involved in before the accountant could take over, etc.

Second, I put each annual filing or task I was personally responsible for in some way into my Google Calendar with a notification set a week in advance (or whatever lead-time I needed to make it happen) so that I would get an email AND a pop-up notification on my devices to remind me (all of them).

Without fail these reminders always take me by surprise.

—

More complex problems and tasks often require more complex solutions, and thereby involve more of an investment ahead of time to systemize. Again, in some cases this involves and overlaps with the Basic Skill of Pre-Doing, though in most cases you aren't able to pre-do the work, you're just systemizing it in a way that will make it much easier for you to do later and / or to delegate to someone else. So though it can cost you some time up front, you will potentially end up saving yourself UNBELIEVABLE amounts of time and effort down the road.

For example, try re-learning how to do an annual filing for the Quebec government when all of the documentation is only available in French and not even your 100% fluent-in-French wife can understand what it says. Guess how many years in a row she wants to be asked to be involved in untangling that web?

Zero years in a row, that's how many.

Obviously there's an enormous amount of variation here with the Systemized 20, but let's math it out anyway to see where it takes us...

| MATH TIME – 200X

The most straightforward way to think of the numerical value of the Systemized 20 is the re-application of the 80 / 20 Principle, or a generalized 4x improvement of your productivity. It makes sense logically if you consider that you can apply systemization in some way to about 80% of your tasks, which is why I use the term Systemized 20, instead of just saying "systemization".

YOU: "Isn't that just counting that *same* 4x value from the 80 / 20 Principle over again?"

Nope, because originally you're using the 80 / 20 Principle to REMOVE work entirely. You're just not doing it (at all) because you've decided it doesn't matter enough. And then perhaps even applying that principle again to do even less of the original work (20 of 20).

But if you then take that remaining 4-20% and systemize your response to 80% of it, or as much of it as you can imagine, you see a *new* 4x savings.

YOU: "My brain hurts."

Yep, and that's why there are so many warnings at the beginning of this book. All of these things are real and have real implications for the velocity with which you experience life. Here's how we're stacking up now, making this 4x a multiple (not using addition like we did with the first few hacks):

Normal 80 / 20 Principle = 4x in Productivity

Parkinson's 20 = 10x in Productivity

20 of 20 = 16x in Productivity

Parkinson's 20 of 20 = 20x in Productivity

Synergized Parkinson's 20 of 20 = 50x in Productivity

Systemized & Synergized Parkinson's 20 of 20 = 200x in Productivity

| IMPORTANT NOTE

Systemization is one of the more freeing techniques that are covered in this book. I decided to add it here because at this point, you're going to be experiencing some speed-friction issues. If you're following along with these in your real life, you might need the relief.

Because you are already going way, way too fast.

Systemization will help you to not die or go to jail.

—

But we're not quite done, and the next (and final) hack is going to require that you're EXTREMELY on top of this systemization thing. Make sure you have this down pat before going any further.

We're going to try and leave the planet with this next one...

—

| ACTION STEP

What is one thing you have to do each day, month, or year that you can immediately systemize so that in the future, instead of taking hours, it will only take minutes (or seconds!) to complete?

Motivation is everything. You can do the work of two people, but you can't be two people. Instead, you have to inspire the next guy down the line and get him to inspire his people.

- Lee Iacocca

Hack #7

Extended 20

It's 2016 and I'm talking through a project with someone I work with at church. I'm sort of in a coaching role with them, so it's a regular meeting, and there's this thing that they've got to do. (I'm generalizing quite a bit because this story is true like 20 times over, with a dozen different people and different projects this past year.)

I'm working to help them see the 20% that matters most and giving them "intellectual permission" to drop the rest and move onto the next task.

Often these are projects that originally started with me, or that were assigned to me and that I systemized, boiled down the bare 10-20% that mattered most, and then trained and handed off to another staff person, volunteer, or contract in one of the organizations I'm connected with.

Trim

Systemize

Delegate

I'm doing this at home, at work, and at church all the time now, and I call it the Extended 20.

| HACK #7 - EXTENDED 20

The Extended 20 is where you take the principles that you've picked up in this book and press them out into the world around you. This takes two forms:

1. Delegating - Systemizing and trimming work so that it can be safely put into the hands of other people, leaving you with only a supervisory relationship towards the original work.

2. Discipling - Passing on these basic & advanced productivity hacks to increase the output of those whom you are supervising or working with.

With the above you are first seeking to extend your own work capacity through delegation (this may be through hiring employees, training volunteers, or even project sharing with co-workers) and then further extend it again by helping your supervisees (or co-workers) to maximize their own productivity. In as much as you are successful in one or both of these steps, you will greatly expand your own productivity.

YOU: "This feels like cheating."

Nope. If you're looking to hit the upper stratosphere of productivity, that always involves other people: Team work, organizations, companies, these kinds of structures exist because people are able to accomplish more together than they are alone (see original definition of synergy).

That's not to say that it is ALWAYS the case, anyone who has sat on a committee knows that grouping people together around a task or responsibility can actually slow things way, way down. But generally speaking, if you want to move mountains all the time, you have to be a part of a larger structure.

REALITY CHECK - This is CEO type stuff. I'm not advocating that you start doing corporate retreat type "trust-fall exercises" with your family after dinner (though that could be fun?), but I *am* saying that if you are looking to experience the 1,000x type productivity that the title of this book promises, you're going to have to gather some folks together to form a larger organism.

Otherwise 1,000x type productivity will kill the host (you).

—

Regardless if you are running a Fortune 500 company now or simply have aspirations of doing so, most of us participate in some form of community or tribal structures, and can see some immediate benefits from the basic application of the Extended 20 hack.

Let's look at an example of each type of extension...

| EXAMPLE #1 - DELEGATING

About two years into our e-commerce business, we were ready for a real vacation. But as many self-employed people quickly realize, we couldn't really leave. No one was coming to rescue us; it was up to us to keep all the juggling balls in the air all the time.

We could do *some* of the work from anywhere: update the website, communicate with customers, etc., but the real sticking point was fulfilling orders. For that we had to be near our fulfillment office (which at that time was also known as our bedroom). We had enough orders coming in at that time that I needed to go to the post office three times a week (M-W-F usually).

We did eventually find that we could put a notice up on our website saying we're going to be late by a week on fulfilling orders because we were at the beach with our kids, here's a 15% off discount code (BEACH15!) for you to enjoy as compensation, etc., and that worked out usually. People were happy to get a deal and seemed to appreciate that we had kids we needed to spend time with. But any longer than that and we'd risk losing customers (and then have no money for food or rent).

Additionally I was finding it hard to keep the business going smoothly. I'd order more product, put it into our inventory, generate a big pulse of sales, get really busy doing fulfillment and customer service, and then only notice when everything slowed back down that we had run out a bunch of items and would remember / have time to do an inventory update and re-order. Despite being a super-productive person, there just wasn't time to do it all, and it was limiting our growth in a big way.

So for those two reasons (not being able to get away and not being able to do it all myself with the ideal level of focus) we decided we needed to hire help. That in itself was a big leap of faith, to bring someone on and pay them meant a major new expense, but more than that, we realized we couldn't have them working out of our bedroom (awkward when they want to get an early start on the day) so we had to ALSO take a leap of faith by renting out a second apartment down the street to use as an office.

Craziness.

But the bet paid off, and today we have a larger office with even more people involved, and some even working from other time zones. In fact I'm in Ireland right now as I am putting the finishing polish on this book, and looking out at a pasture full of sheep. How? Because we have systemized, trimmed, and delegated things out for our business to the point where we can basically live anywhere in the world and continue to work on the undelegated portions via the Internet.

Delegation has allowed me to exponentially increase the amount of work I "accomplish", both directly and indirectly through management or supervision. It has had a more significant impact on our daily experience of life than any other idea already covered in this book.

To make it this far has involved an ENORMOUS amount of work: years of building systems, optimizing them, finding and training good people, figuring out how to have the right amount and kind of oversight, and when to move responsibilities around. But delegation is the kind of work that pays big dividends over time, and is eminently worth the effort.

There are excellent books out there on how to do this well so I won't expand on it further here, only to say that delegation is integral to taking things to the next level.

And almost equally important is the second step: discipling.

| EXAMPLE #2 - DISCIPLING

Discipling is allowing others to pattern their life after your own. For this to be a positive thing, you need to have learned and internalized something useful, something that others would love to learn and emulate. In our case I'm hoping that the principles you're learning in this book will be something that others can learn from and emulate as well, especially if they are persons whom you are actively delegating work to.

The illustration on the cover of this book shows a man strapped to a single-stage rocket. Delegating to people who are only working with a nominal level of productivity isn't going to make a huge difference for your life. The amount of work it takes to systemize and hand it off and then supervise them over the long run may end up costing you about as much time as you're saving. Things might work out this way because they're just the wrong person for the job, or maybe you did a poor job of systemizing or training. Regardless of the reason, delegating alone doesn't always result in a net gain. (Hence the old adage, "If you want something done right, do it yourself.")

The real magic happens when you've done those things right AND you've disciplined them in productivity. Then you're looking at being strapped to a *multistage* rocket, which is really what you need if you're going to escape the earth's gravity and reach the very highest levels of productivity.

What does this look like?

Every time I screen-capture a training session with someone, they want to know what I'm doing and why I'm doing it (see example of Pre-Doing back in chapter 7). And *every* time I explain that it's so I never have to personally give the same training again, and as I say this, I can almost see this little explosion go off in their head. Literally hundreds of hours of their future lives have just been freed up from the mundane task of re-training people on the same thing, over and over again (and sometimes having to re-give the same material over again with the SAME person who seems to have forgotten how to do it).

In this way, discipling is easy. If what you're doing is magic, whomever you're working with is going to love it and pick it up on their own. You're not going to have to force them to start doing it.

—

YOU: "But does this really end up making such a huge difference? Seriously, 1,000x?"

Well let's look at the math together and see...

| MATH TIME - 1,000X

If you systemize and delegate the most important and potent 4% of your work down to a layer of "supervised work", where you're simply overseeing and / or coaching the person doing the actual work, your personal involvement in the work drops to under 1%. If you teach them to personally apply all of the principles in this book, and manage (theoretically) to get their own productivity up to 100x of what is normal, and you supervise 10 people like this each week, your own *extended* productivity skyrockets into the four-digit range (1,000x or more).

I use the figures of 10 people X 100x* = 1,000x because that is about the number of people that I am interacting with on peak weeks, and that I could theoretically boost up to if all everything aligned and circumstances necessitated that level of ridiculousness. That said, I cannot explicitly state that it has ever objectively occurred, though I imagine that I have gotten pretty close on more than one occasion.

*Note that I'm using only HALF of the potential 200x that I could be achieving on my own, without extending it out into other people. The reality is that once you start delegating, it's not as necessary (or even possible?) that you can be hitting 200x. You can more-easily hit 500x or 1,000x or even 2,000x with other people involved in your work than just doing 200x on your own and dying.

What is it that you can legally and ethically systemize and delegate away to someone else from your current workload? That might mean paying someone to mow your lawn or do your laundry, realizing you can bill more hours and make more money even with the added expense of their services.

Or it might mean delegating some of your billable work, so that you can take the time to mow the lawn yourself because you need the exercise, outdoor time, and Vitamin D producing sunshine exposure.

It cuts either way. The point is that you have new options when you open your mind to *delegation*. And not just delegating, but cutting it down first to only the 20 of the 20 and putting a Parkinson's Law limitation on the work, and helping them to see how they can *synergize* their work, rolling one project into the next.

| IMPORTANT NOTE

Again, before you attempt to push all of this stuff onto the people you live and work with, take some time to internalize it and live it out. The reality is you can rarely force the people around you to be more productive.

However you CAN allow them to see the effects of these principles in your life, lead by example, and make them WANT to know more.

Also keep in mind that everyone is going to apply these in slightly different ways, and see a different level of results. Some people will NEVER 10x their work, it's just not in them, because they work differently, and that's OK. Be careful not to actually LOWER your team's productivity by making them into something they're not.

1. Use these to their best effect in your own life.

2. Be open about how you work and increase your own productivity

3. Share and teach these principles with an open hand, allowing those around you to pick up on them and choose if and when to ask for more.

—

If you've applied all of these principles, you're now doing what I call the *Extended, Synergized, & Systemized Parkinson's 20 of 20.* That's the maximum you can get out of these when they're all rolled together and pressed down into your life and into the lives of those around you.

You've made it.

You've learned it all.

Now there are only two paths before you:

1. Hurtle through Time & Space and Die Horribly

2. Find Balance & Peace in the utilization of these principles

Before we end, I'm going to try and help you find the right path...

—

| ACTION STEPS

Who's the most important person in your life with whom you could share this book and its principles?

How much can you raise your personal productivity by using an Extended 20 and sharing these principles with your team?

Every poem should remind the reader that they are going to die.

- Edgar Allan Poe

Epilogue

It's 1987 and I'm playing in the sandbox in my backyard with my brother. We're bringing buckets of water from the spigot to give the sand the structural stability it needs to maintain tunnels for our Matchbox cars. It's sunny out, the sky is blue, the grass is green, and I don't have a care in the world.

I am 100% engrossed with making sand tunnels.

Most of us have similar memories, of carefree childhood moments, in which we remember a feeling of focus and abandon that seems somehow unattainable in modern life. With Smartphones and Email and Facebook, there are very few carefree moments left. Even our few outdoor excursions are dominated by the ever-watching eye of social media and the almost irresistible impulse to capture and broadcast every "adventurous" moment for the self-worshiping acquisition of little blue thumbs.

You want to 1,000x that kind of life? No way. So let's attempt to take the "Scary" out of going Fast. Below is the one principle that I use to find balance in the utilization of an *Extended, Synergized, & Systemized Parkinson's 20 of 20*.

All of the benefits.

None of the panic attacks.

| DON'T FILL IN THE GAPS

As you utilize these principles, you'll find that you have MORE time to do *new* things, thereby gaining in your overall productivity. Resist the urge to fill in everything and instead allow that space to be free time to do other things (go outside, spend time with family, read science fiction, etc.).

Put plainly: *Don't fill in the gaps!*

This simple principle is easy to understand but hard to implement. It's hard because when you're getting so much done and going so fast, it's hard to pull up for a moment and rest and just DO NOTHING.

If you struggle at all with doing nothing now, imagine how much harder it will be when you're experiencing 100-1000x productivity levels? When you're supervising 5-10 people who are also being super productive and are looking to you for decisions on MASSIVE movements of work?

That kind of environment will sweep away any little notations in your calendar to take "personal time".

You have to be AS AGGRESSIVE about carving out rest and outdoor time and family time as you have been about maximizing your productivity. You need an equal force to press against those productivity forces. You may need to set up accountability in this area, and press in a measure of self-discipline to NOT maximize, synergize, systemize, and extend all of your daily activities.

CHOOSE not to delegate EVERYTHING.

CHOOSE not to brush your teeth while using the toilet.

CHOOSE not to eat dinner while using your laptop on the treadmill and live-casting your multitasking on Facebook for little blue thumbs.*

*Not a true story.

—

This book could be a lot longer. I could have spent more time on it. But the reality is you've got your 20%, thank you very much, and I think you're going to get the 80% of what you needed out of this. I won't waste anymore of your time by padding this up with a bunch of extra stuff to read.

Even now I'm just writing this to have some kind of "conclusion"...probably a waste of your time, sorry.

Get out there and get started.

But mind your gauges...

| ACTION STEP

Block out one day a week as your "Sabbath Rest" day. Refuse to do anything of lasting "work-value" (e.g., Eat candy and play video games with your kids / friends / family).

ME: "Enjoy this book? Consider leaving a review!"

YOU: "I don't know...I'm pretty busy."

ME: "Don't you love being able to read reviews that help you make wise purchases on Amazon?"

YOU: "Well...yes."

ME: "Be that hero! Write a really great review and help someone else make a good decision."

YOU: "..."

ME: "Or any kind of review. Even a review of meager effort on your part."

YOU: "That sounds more doable. I just don't like all the pressure."

ME: "No problem. Anything is fine."

YOU: "Fine, I'll do it tomorrow."

ME: "What? Why not do it today?"

YOU: "Fine."

ME: "Why not do it right NOW?"

YOU: "FINE!"

YOU: (going to do review on Amazon...)

YOU: (coming back unsuccessful) "I can't find your book."

ME: "Easy, just go to BrianMichaelStegner.com and that'll take you right to my author page, and all of my books will be there."

YOU: "You have other books?"

ME: "Oh yes, but don't get distracted. Write that review first!"

Brian Michael Stegner (1979-) was born in Albany, New York, grew up in Portland, Oregon, and attended college in Chicago and Saskatchewan. Primarily a storyteller, Brian specializes in 'Dry-fi', a mashup of literary fiction, nonfiction, science fiction, and dry humor. When not writing, he divides his time between family, church planting, entrepreneurial ventures, coaching, and reluctantly traveling the world.

He lives in Montreal, Québec with his wife and kids.

www.ingramcontent.com/pod-product-compliance
Lightning Source LLC
Chambersburg PA
CBHW031425210526
45464CB00005B/2061